Mom's Genes

by Shannon Pulaski

Illustrated by Zach Wideman

Dear Stephanie,
Be brave!
Be fierce!
Be strong ♡
Sincerely,
Shannon

ISBN 978-0-9997666-0-6

For Brooke, Riley, & Luke – To the moon.

Mom loves to tell me all about what
went into the making of me;

Mom's, Dad's, Grandma's, and Pop's
genes are how I came to be.

Deep inside my body are cells that hold the recipe,
my DNA carries the genes from my ancestry.

There are instructions in each and every gene
that teach my body to work like a well-oiled machine.

Some genes can turn your eyes blue
and put freckles on your nose.

Some genes can make
your hair curly

and give you big
bubbly toes.

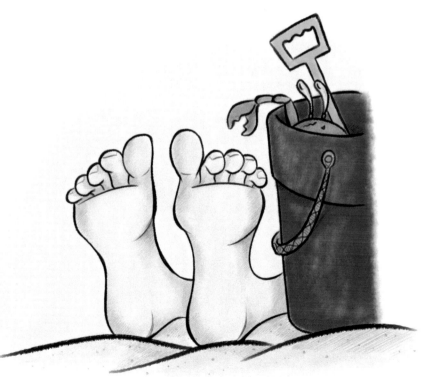

My Pop's genes grew him to be almost seven feet tall.

My brother's genes make him good at throwing a ball.

Last week at the dentist, I had a cavity;
Mom chuckled and said, "It runs in our family."

Other genes can make it hard to stay healthy and might make you sick.

You may need the help of a doctor to give your body a little kick.

That is why my cousin needs to take her medicine every night,

and why mom's surgery left scars from her cancer fight.

Mom tells me her
genes make her

brave, fierce,
and strong...

...and that we learn from the stories that are passed along.

Mom says learning our
history will help me to see

that knowing myself is the key to staying healthy.

Paying attention to how my body feels day to day will remind me to tell my doctor if something feels astray.

Lucky for me I'll be able to share

the story of my genes...

so my family can help me understand what it all means.

Your family tree can be a guide to the body's maze that is deep inside.

Ask your mom, ask your dad, ask your grandpa, too,

OUR FAMILY TREE

to discover what genes are inside of you!

GENE-ius Word #1

DNA

DNA is material in our cells that we inherit from our parents. It is a molecule that gives our cells instruction on how to make proteins that help our bodies work and look the way they do.

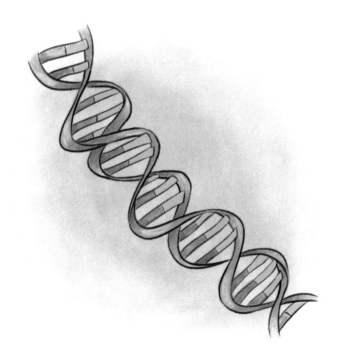

Genes

Genes are part of our DNA and determine
what traits we inherit from our parents.

Ancestry

Ancestry is your family's history
of relatives that came before you.